THEN & NOW

DERBY AND ANSONIA

The historical society would like to dedicate this book to the memory of Clara Barton Drew. Born Clara Barton Tomlinson in Seymour, Connecticut, on November 25, 1867, she was named after Red Cross founder Clara Barton. Moving to Ansonia as a young girl, she married John Wilbur Drew in 1888 and resided on New Street. A pioneer among female photographers, Mrs. Drew operated a photography studio out of her New Street home for decades, and her work graces this book (including the cover), as well as *Ansonia,* in Arcadia Publishing's Images of America series. Mrs. Drew became friends with her namesake Clara Barton, who visited her New Street home several times. Clara Barton Drew died on February 21, 1946.

THEN & NOW

DERBY AND ANSONIA

Derby Historical Society

ARCADIA

Copyright © 2004 by Derby Historical Society
ISBN 0-7385-3688-1

First published 2004

Published by Arcadia Publishing,
Charleston SC, Chicago IL, Portsmouth NH, San Francisco CA

Printed in Great Britain

Library of Congress Catalog Card Number: 2004109815

For all general information, contact Arcadia Publishing:
Telephone 843-853-2070
Fax 843-853-0044
E-mail sales@arcadiapublishing.com
For customer service and orders:
Toll-free 1-888-313-2665

Visit us on the Internet at www.arcadiapublishing.com

CONTENTS

ACKNOWLEDGMENTS

As with the two Images of America books that the Derby Historical Society published in 1999, the primary caption author of *Derby and Ansonia* was executive director Robert Novak Jr. With a few noted exceptions, all of the "now" photographs were taken in 2004 by the society's curator, Marian O'Keefe.

Most of the "then" photographs come from the Derby Historical Society's own archives, though it should be noted that others were donated or borrowed from Edward M. Tackach, Randy Ritter, Vincent "Jim" Giammario, Markanthony Izzo, Elizabeth Dearborn, and Joan Driscoll. Other pictures came from the Ansonia Public Library, the Derby Public Library, the Pasquale Pepe collection, and others.

Those who assisted in the production of the book, either with information or assistance, include David Carver, John Doherty, Terence O'Keefe, Mary Ann Capone of the Ansonia Public Library, and Danielle Basilicata. We extend our thanks to all who enriched the quality of *Derby and Ansonia* through their assistance.

Primary written sources included the *History of Derby, Connecticut, 1642–1880* (1880), by Rev. Samuel Orcutt and Dr. Ambrose Beardsley, and the *Tercentenary Pictorial and History of the Lower Naugatuck Valley* (1935), by Leo Molloy. *Valley Downtowns: A Historical Perspective* (1980), by the Valley Regional Planning Agency, was also very helpful, as was the Derby Historical Society's *Survey of Valley Architecture* (1964), by Marian O'Keefe. Other sources included *Derby 300th Anniversary Commemorative Book 1675–1975*; *A History of Ansonia, Bicentennial–1976*; *Ansonia 100th Anniversary 1889–1989 Souvenir Book and Program*; and *Commemorating Ansonia's Incorporation as Connecticut's 168th City* (1993).

The now defunct newspapers *Derby Transcript* and *Ansonia Evening Sentinel* were also invaluable reference sources, as were numerous years of the Ansonia and Derby local directories. Both souvenir history pamphlets published by the *Derby Transcript* in 1896—Ansonia as well as Derby and Shelton—were invaluable, as was *Illustrated Review of the Naugatuck Valley* (1890), published by Sovereign Publishing.

INTRODUCTION

With this book, the Derby Historical Society proudly releases its third Arcadia Publishing title in five years, *Derby and Ansonia*, this one in the Then and Now series. Founded in 1946, the Derby Historical Society is a dynamic regional historical group that now serves as the primary historical society for Derby and Ansonia. The society also, from a regional standpoint, embraces the rest of the Lower Naugatuck Valley towns that were once part of—or whose history was dramatically influenced by—the original Derby settlement.

One of the most frequently asked questions we received after publishing the Images of America titles *Derby* and *Ansonia* in 1999 was, "Where was this photograph taken?" Even though the description was often included in the books, we found that many people had a hard time envisioning the location of many of the historic scenes. A major reason was that the cities of Derby and Ansonia have changed dramatically over the years, particularly in the wake of the 1955 flood and subsequent redevelopment projects.

The Derby Historical Society is particularly blessed with an extensive archive of local historical photographs, the result of over half a century of collecting and donations. Even now, we still receive new photographs to further enrich our collection. These photographs tell the story of the valley's evolution, from then to now. The purpose of this book is to chronicle many of the changes, and even some facets of the cities that have not changed, through comparing and contrasting historic photographs with modern-day images taken in 2004.

To that end, the society's curator, Marian O'Keefe, took great pains to match as precisely as possible the exact spots where the historic photographs were taken. In some cases, this meant she had to scout parking lots to find now vanished streets and buildings. In other cases, this meant she had to risk life and limb dodging traffic on major thoroughfares that were once quiet country lanes. The results of these efforts speak for themselves in the pages of this book.

The city of Derby is the historic heart of the Lower Naugatuck Valley, while the city of Ansonia is its geographic heart, as well as its largest population center. Along with Seymour and Oxford, the two cities were once the same town. The historic Colonial center of Derby actually straddled the east side of the Naugatuck River.

From this Colonial center radiated two factory villages, as they were called then: Birmingham, where downtown Derby is today, and Ansonia. By the mid-19th century, these were three distinct communities. But after Ansonia's growth dictated that it break from Derby and form its own city, the historic Colonial center was partitioned between the two in 1889. Meanwhile, Birmingham was absorbed into the greater city of Derby in 1894. Thus, from the common root—Derby's old Colonial center—sprang the modern day cities of Derby and Ansonia. This helps explain why the Derby Historical Society's headquarters, the David Humphreys House, is located near the town line in Ansonia, while it draws membership from and operates extensively in both cities.

While the twin cities have evolved into their own distinct character and identities, in many ways there is still cooperation and collaboration between them, as well as a friendly rivalry that seems to become acute during football season. Despite all this, their common historical ties should not be forgotten, and many of the historic pictures contained in this book were taken before, or not long after, the separation of 1889.

While we thank many people who contributed to this book on the previous page, it would be most fitting if we thanked those who have helped or supported the historical society over the years. Without this support, books such as this would not be possible, to say nothing of the houses and historical collections we preserve and our educational programs. Because of the joint support given by the people of Ansonia and Derby, the society itself has evolved into a dynamic entity that today serves both cities and the surrounding region.

Robert J. Novak Jr., Executive Director
Marian K. O'Keefe, Curator
Derby Historical Society
July 9, 2004

This is the view that greeted people entering Derby's business section from the train stations and East Derby along Main Street. The photograph was taken in the 1880s in front of the Hoffman Hotel. The building with the columns on the right, just past the carriages, was the headquarters of the Ousatonic Water Company, which built the Ousatonic Dam across the Housatonic River in 1870.

The original Derby settlement was located on the east bank of the Naugatuck River, both above and below the present Derby-Ansonia town line. Because the Housatonic River was navigable from here to Long Island Sound, shipping was an early valley industry. This view, taken by Clara Barton Drew, looks north from East Derby. The barges on the right are moored at the foot of Commerce Street. The Naugatuck River branches to Ansonia above that, and beyond the Naugatuck is Birmingham, now downtown Derby. Sullivan's Island is in the middle of the river, with Shelton on the left bank. When shipping declined in the early 1800s, waterpower from the rivers was used for

manufacturing, and the industrial communities of Birmingham and Ansonia grew from the original Derby settlement. Most boats that ply the Housatonic today are pleasure craft.

Chapter 1

EAST DERBY

John W. Barber engraved this woodcut in 1836, showing how Derby Landing, also called Derby Narrows, presented itself to travelers from New Haven. At the time, the village was composed of 50 houses, 5 stores, a number of shops, and 2 churches. On the horizon, Birmingham in its infancy is visible, as is the covered bridge that led to Huntington, now Shelton. The road Barber used 168 years ago is now called Old New Haven Road, overlooking New Haven Avenue, or Route 34, the new main road to the Elm City. Prospect Street still winds up the hill to the right, just as it did in 1836. The trees now hide the Housatonic River from view.

The Causeway, as the Main Street bridge over the Naugatuck River was called when this photograph was taken in the early 1900s, was one of the busiest thoroughfares in the valley in terms of pedestrians, carriages, and trolleys. The Causeway was situated between two train stations, and the Junction was located in the distance at the corner. After the flood of 1955, the new bridge was erected below the old, damaged one. Notice the St. Michael's steeple to the right of the old bridge below, while the church is now at the head of the new intersection in the present-day photograph. The road at the end of the bridge, Front Street, was much closer to the riverbank but no longer exists.

Derby Junction, Conn. Trolley Terminus

Another view of Main and Front Streets shows why it was called the Junction. The trolley to the left connects to Bridgeport via Shelton and downtown Derby. The trolley in the center background connects with Waterbury via Ansonia. The trolley in the right foreground connects to New Haven via East Derby and the Yale Bowl. This was one of the few places in Connecticut where trolleys going to all three of its major western cities could be found. Now one of the busiest intersections in the valley, the area no longer betrays any clues to its former importance to the area's inhabitants a century before.

The northwest view of the Junction shows the Causeway. The area where the Causeway intersected with Derby Avenue is close to where the former Howard Johnson building (Tailgators in 2004) is now located. All of the businesses and apartment buildings that lined the north side of the intersection in the photograph below are long gone. Various business conducted over the years in these structures included confectioneries, taverns, restaurants, barbers, and others.

The Junction, Derby, Conn.

The building in the foreground of this southeast view of the Junction housed Mester's Drugstore for decades. Just behind the horse and carriage, the tracks of the Naugatuck Division of the New York, New Haven and Hartford Railroad cross the trolley tracks. Just south and out of view from where this photograph was taken is the East Derby combination freight and passenger depot, the original of which was built by the Naugatuck Railroad, a predecessor of the New York, New Haven and Hartford, in 1849. The small structure under the left side of St. Michael's is a waiting area for trolley passengers. Only St. Michael's and the retaining wall that supports it survived to be photographed today.

Fronting both Derby Avenue and Bank Street behind it, about half a dozen doors south of St. Michael's, was the elegant Sawyer mansion. In 1902, Franklin School was constructed where it stood, replacing the Gilbert Street School as the primary public school for East Derby. Rather than razing the mansion, workers moved it in three sections to three different locations. Franklin School served Derby until it was closed in the late 1970s. In 1986, it was converted into the condominium units seen from Bank Street in the present-day photograph. Two sections of the Sawyer House stand today: one on Crescent Street and the other on Bank Street.

The house in the foreground is the Andrew Johnson house, built *c.* 1798 on the corner of today's Bank and Gilbert Streets. The house was dismantled in 1928 and reportedly moved to Westchester County, New York. A "modern" home was built shortly thereafter, but note that its three historic neighbors are all still present in the lower photograph. In the left rear is the relocated main frame of the Sawyer mansion. In the background to the right is the old Gilbert Street School, now a private residence. The saltbox on the far right has also survived.

The right portion of the Sawyer mansion was relocated to New Haven Avenue and Commerce Street, where it did not fare as well as the structure's other sections. Located very close to the intersection, it was eventually torn down, and no trace of the corner's former grandeur remains. A careful glance will reveal a number of the old homes in the background across New Haven Avenue have survived the centuries, but they betray little hint to their age or history to the thousands of automobiles that zip by every day.

Marian O'Keefe took this photograph of the historic Commodore Hull House on July 30, 1961, one day before the landmark at 38 Commerce Street was razed. Commodore Hull, who commanded the USS *Constitution* at the famous battle where it earned the nickname "Old Ironsides" during the War of 1812, was born here in 1773. Gen. Joseph Wheeler, who later became a Confederate general, also grew up at this house. The house was torn down to make way for the Derby Coal and Oil Company, and the following January the Derby Historical Society dedicated a plaque that remains on the spot to this day. At the time the lower photograph was taken in 2004, the building that housed Derby Coal and Oil was abandoned.

The three-and-a-half-story Captain Ebenezer Gracey house was built in 1761 at what became 113 New Haven Avenue. Captain Gracey owned 150 feet of river frontage, a wharf, and a warehouse at Derby Narrows. So busy was this section of the Housatonic River that it was nicknamed "New Boston" in the 1760s. Captain Gracey also kept a store along the river with his business partner, a sea captain named Joseph Hull, the commodore's father. The house was perpendicular to the street and overlooked a pond that is still present. When the lower photograph was taken in 1962, a florist operated out of the home, but the house has subsequently razed to make way for the Bradley Pond Professional

Center. One family member, Henry Bradley, was a noted Derby historian. Marian O'Keefe took both photographs.

Behind the carriage is the beautiful Gates homestead, on the corner of Derby Avenue and Bank Street. The Gates family occupied this property from the late 1700s to the 1950s. A generous community benefactor, Frank H. Gates willed the property to the nearby First Congregational Church, stipulating that the home was to be torn down. St. Michael's Church now owns it, though both houses of worship share it. The home in back belonged to Franklin Hallock, owner of F. Hallock Company (on Main Street), until his death in 1890. The Barry family bought the home shortly after. The Derby Gas and Electric Company hired Julia Barry in 1891, and she filled all positions in the utility's office, from clerk to supervisor, before becoming the Derby Gas and Electric Company treasurer in 1929.

The Gates mansion, on Derby Avenue at Banks Street, no longer obstructs the view of First Congregational Church. Founded in 1671, the church is the oldest institution of any kind in the Naugatuck Valley. The present church building was constructed in 1820. Dr. Pinney's home (in the left foreground) now houses St. Michael's Post, Catholic War Veterans, and their parking lot is where the Hallock-Barry home stood. The lot now reveals the law offices that were once the Sidney Downs home (in the background). On August 6, 1887, the Derby Gas and Electric Company installed its first electric streetlights ever on Derby Avenue.

The Claudius Bartelame house was a perfect example of an old saltbox-style home, with a long sloping roof in the rear. Born in France in 1737, Bartelame immigrated to Nova Scotia, where he fought the British. Expelled in 1756 to the American colonies with thousands of other Acadians, he came to Derby in 1760, where he built this house and married a local girl. Bartelame learned English and Anglicized his last name to Bartholomew. His son Jerrod opened fire on the Washington Bridge across the mouth of the Housatonic in 1807. The Washington Bridge was hated in Derby because it hindered local shipping. For many years, Claudius was Derby's only Roman Catholic. After surviving for centuries, the old house was replaced with the present one in the early 20th century.

A fter Derby suffered an economic
depression from the collapse of its
large-scale shipping industry in the
early 19th century, salvation came when
Derby native Sheldon Smith extended a
canal down the west bank of the
Naugatuck River to its terminus with
the Housatonic. Attracted by the
abundant waterpower, industrialists
quickly built factories, and Derby
joined the American Industrial
Revolution. Originally called Second
Street, Main Street soon developed into
the major commercial thoroughfare for
the new "factory village," called
Birmingham, between 1836 and 1891,
as businesses sprouted to support the
industries and their workers. This
c. 1925 view shows the Hoffmann

Chapter 2
MAIN STREET, DERBY

Hotel, at Main and Factory Streets.
Beyond it is the Ousatonic Water
Company headquarters and the three-
story Shelton Block.

The wonderful view above shows the hill on Main Street, between Elizabeth and Bridge Streets, before the area began taking on the trappings of a city. The retaining wall to the right was part of the Donald Judson home, built in 1840, a year after he and a partner relocated the covered bridge over the Housatonic to Hawkins Point, where Bridge Street is now. The Hawkins home is to the left, with Bridge Street between it and the neighboring building. As the lower view shows, everything in the old photograph is long gone, except the hill itself and the streets. Most of the buildings on the right side of the modern photograph are themselves at or approaching a century old.

Until the Commodore Hull Bridge was completed in 1951, Bridge Street was the only gateway to Derby for foot and vehicular traffic from Shelton and the rest of Fairfield County. Older residents still recall the bridge jammed with Shelton residents every Friday evening to shop on Main Street. The tall building with the peaked roof behind the right side of the trolley was called the Loomer Block. Next to it was a four-story wood-framed building. The Howard and Barber department store winds around the curve. The modern photograph, taken in 2000 by Markanthony Izzo of Derby, shows that the intersection is still the gateway to Derby, although the Loomer Block, Howard and Barber, and several other Main Street buildings were demolished for redevelopment in 2003.

MAIN & BRIDGE STREETS

The last covered bridge on Bridge
Street lasted from 1857 until 1891.
The bridge was a toll bridge until Derby
and Shelton bought it in 1875, after
threatening to build a new free bridge
right next to it if the owners did not
sell. A lattice walkway was built along
the bridge's south side in 1878, and the
fact it does not appear in the older
photograph shows that the photograph
predates that year. An iron bridge
replaced the covered bridge in 1891. The
iron bridge, in turn, was replaced in
1919 by the concrete one that still exists
today. The building with the furniture
warehouse sign still exists as of this
writing, housing Hubbell Brothers
Shoes. Founded in 1896, Hubbell's is
Connecticut's oldest shoe store.

This interesting view of Main Street was taken from the foot of Elizabeth Street after the blizzard of 1888. The four-and-a-half-story Loomer Block is in the center of the photograph. Lyman Loomer ran a stagecoach to New Haven here in the late 1840s. The original section of Howard and Barber is two doors to the right of the Loomer Block. The section of the building that wound around the corner was added later. To the left of the Loomer Block was a bakery that was later replaced by a more substantial brick structure seen in the photograph taken in 2003, just before demolition began on the building, as well as Loomer, Howard and Barber, and other Main Street buildings. The building on the extreme left in the present-day picture once housed Woolworth's.

The three-story building on the corner of Main and Elizabeth Streets, the two-story building next to it, and the third building beyond it with a peaked parapet were collectively known as Hull's Block. The first building with the round parapet was called Somer's Block, while the second, lower building with the rounded parapet was the Brush Block. On January 12, 1879, a terrible fire destroyed the third building of Hull's Block, Somer's Block, and Mr. Hull's home behind them fronting Elizabeth Street, and damaged the rest of the block. The damaged buildings were repaired, and the destroyed ones were replaced. The entire block was demolished in 1976 to make way for the Derby Savings Bank's new headquarters. Derby Savings Bank was founded in 1846.

Another view of the now vanished block on Main Street between Elizabeth and Minerva Streets sometime after the 1879 fire shows the corner building of Hull's Block virtually unchanged. The block's second building now has a third floor, while the third building of Hull's Block and former Somer's Block have both been replaced. All were razed in 1976. Across the street, the wood-framed former Crofut Hotel appears in the right foreground, while one of the oldest buildings on Main Street, Nathan's Hall (built in 1845) is the long brick building in the right background. Until the Sterling Opera House was completed in 1889, this was Derby's main meeting hall and gathering place, and like Sterling it once housed town offices.

MAIN STREET, DERBY, CONN.

Main Street Derby was a bustling commercial center when this photograph was taken *c.* 1895. The trolley proceeding up the hill, just above Caroline Street, was part of the "belt line" that connected Derby with Ansonia. Main Street still bustles today, but like many downtown areas, most of the traffic now drives through town, rather than stopping, and many of the old buildings have fallen victim to spates of urban redevelopment. The trolleys are long gone, and traffic now zooms over Main Street along the Route 8 expressway, seen in the background of the lower photograph. In May 2004, not long after the photograph to the left was taken, the former Derby Pizza House (the building with the peaked roof behind and to the left of the trolley) was razed.

The former Derby Pizza House, at the corner of Main and Caroline Streets, is the first building on the left in the lower photograph. Parking was not the challenge it is today. The fact that the Shelton Block does not appear in the photograph below indicates that it was taken before 1875. That year, Edward N. Shelton, owner of the Shelton Tack Company, constructed the three-story brick building in the newer photograph. Called the Shelton Block, it housed the *Derby Transcript* until that paper folded in 1902, and because of this the building was also called the Transcript Block. An enclosed catwalk still connects the building to the original tack factory, which is behind it, off Factory Street.

For over a century, the F. Hallock hardware store was a Derby staple on the corner of Main and Factory Streets. Franklin Hallock was the son of Zephaniah Hallock. Along with their father, Franklin and his brother were Derby's most prominent shipbuilders. The Hallocks launched the last large vessel built in Derby, the *Modesty,* in 1867. The hardware business continued for many decades after Franklin's death in 1890. Branch stores were opened until the Great Depression forced them to close, leaving just the main store in operation. The trucks lined up in front of the store along Main Street's cobblestones are part of a promotion for Maytag washing machines. The store was razed decades ago, and Housatonic Lumber now occupies the corner.

One of Derby's pioneer industries, the Birmingham Iron Foundry was established in 1836. The company continued to grow and expand for nearly a century before it merged with Ansonia's Farrel Foundry and Machine Company in 1927, the combined entity called Farrel-Birmingham. The massive complex became a prominent Derby landmark, at one time employing thousands of people. The Derby branch closed in 1997, and it was razed in 1999. Taking advantage of the cloverleaf at nearby exit 15 off Route 8, the Home Depot was built on the site to a unique design. The Main Street side, seen in the upper photograph, has a brick facing that blends in with the neighborhood, while the rear, which is visible from Route 8, has more of a traditional facade for that home improvement store.

Although technically the whitewashed works of the Sterling Piano complex were not on Main Street, they were located in what is now the Home Depot's parking lot. Once one of Derby's busiest factories, the complex manufactured high-quality pianos, organs, and later player pianos from 1845 to 1926. Note the factory is on a slight embankment. The field in the foreground was called Derby Meadows. Stretching about a mile along the Naugatuck's west bank, the Meadows formed an undeveloped physical barrier between Derby and East Derby, due to frequent flooding. Modern flood controls now make Home Depot's parking lot and Derby's police station, constructed in 1990, relatively safe from flooding, and Route 8 follows the Meadow's former course.

A lling's New Block was completed at the foot of Elizabeth Street in 1896, the same year that the Hubbell Brothers shoe store set up shop. They remained until *c.* 1975, when the corner was razed for redevelopment, moving a block down Main Street, just above where the original Alling's Block once stood at Main and Bridge Streets. Elizabeth Street linked Derby's social center (built around its green, with its business center on Main Street) and as such was a busy thoroughfare. The trolley belt line passed the entire length of the street. John Clouse laid out the Birmingham (now downtown Derby) streets in the 1830s. Elizabeth, Caroline, and Minerva Streets are named after Birmingham founder Sheldon Smith's daughters, while Anson and Olivia Streets are named after his business partner Anson Phelps and his wife.

Chapter 3

ELIZABETH STREET

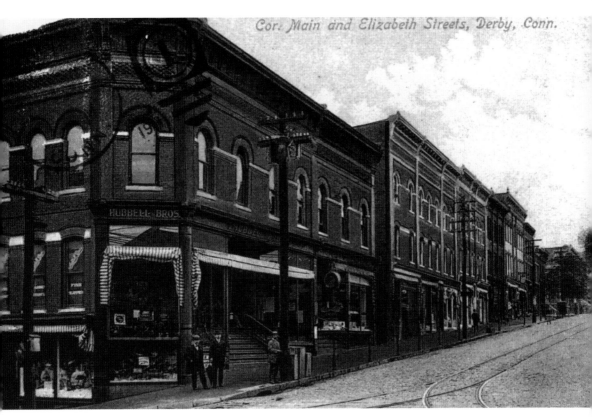

Cor. Main and Elizabeth Streets, Derby, Conn.

This entire block of Elizabeth Street, from Main to Third Streets, fell to redevelopment in the 1970s. Harding Drug Store, the Southern New England Telephone Company, the offices of Dr. Thomas Plunkett, the Birmingham Water Company, the Derby Gas and Electric Company, Green's five-and-dime store, the A&P, and Yudkin Auto Supplies all lined this side of the street when this photograph was taken in the 1920s. The TEAM building and a municipal parking garage seen in the lower photograph now occupy the site.

The photograph to the right was taken on June 21, 1915, at the corner of Elizabeth and Third Streets, apparently after the elm tree on the corner was saved after being diseased or damaged. The corner building that housed the Direct Import Company later was Scarpa Brothers Electrical Store. Today it is better known as the United Cigar convenience store and newsstand. Note the buildings and activity along Third Street. Most of the structures between Elizabeth and Minerva Streets on this side of Third Street, behind United Cigar, are now gone.

Another view of the elm tree at Elizabeth and Third on June 21, 1915, this one taken from the rear of what is now United Cigar, looking toward Elizabeth Street. Third Street continued past Elizabeth and Olivia Streets, all the way to Housatonic Avenue, today's Roosevelt Drive, when the above photograph was taken. Most of the buildings beyond Elizabeth were tenements. Third Street was discontinued between Elizabeth and Olivia Streets when the municipal parking garage was built in the 1970s as part of downtown redevelopment.

This is the north side of Third Street in a view looking toward Elizabeth Street. The stone house on the corner of Minerva and Third Streets was the Samuel Brush home. Derby had a number of stone houses and buildings, many of which survive to this day. Samuel Brush founded a small dry goods store on Main Street in 1859, which quickly expanded. The business was taken over by Howard and Barber in 1884, eight years after Brush's death. A barn on the Brush property served as Birmingham's first firehouse in 1837. The gas station, which takes up the entire block of Third Street in the upper photograph, betrays no hint to the structures that once occupied this busy neighborhood. Marian O'Keefe took both photographs.

Continuing up Elizabeth Street, the block between Third and Fourth Streets marked its transition into Derby's social and cultural center. The peaked house in the left foreground belonged to Dr. Ambrose Beardsley, who employed Ebenezer Basset at one time. Basset grew up in Derby and became the nation's first African American ambassador to a foreign country, which was Haiti. The four-story building next door was called the Bassett House, Derby's premier restaurant and hotel until it burned down in 1911. Narrow Fourth Street passes between the Bassett House and Sterling Opera House in the above photograph, and beyond is the spire of Second Congregational Church. Everything south of Sterling is now changed, with a bank and courthouse now fronting the block.

Known as City Park, Birmingham Green, Public Square, and Derby Green over the years, the green between Elizabeth, Minerva, Fourth, and Fifth Streets evolved into the heart of Derby's social scene in the 19th century, with three churches, desirable residences, and the Bassett and Sterling Opera Houses surrounding it. Birmingham had a law requiring landowners to build on property within a year of purchase in order to prevent land speculation. The green was set aside as an oasis in the midst of the rapidly developing city. Although the public well seen below is gone, a drinking fountain now marks where it was. Many of the walkways through the green are over a century and a half old.

After the Bassett House was lost to fire in 1911, the Hotel Clark was built in its place on Elizabeth and Fourth Streets. The Clark continued Bassett Hotel's legacy of being Derby's premier hotel and restaurant. It was razed in 1969. Fourth Street ran between the Clark and Sterling Opera House to Olivia Street, as well as along the lower end of the green to Minerva Street, but both of these blocks have been discontinued in favor of a public walkway. The bandstand in the old photograph is probably for a parade, while the modern gazebo was added in the 1990s.

The Sterling Opera House was completed in April 1889. Its first play was entitled *Drifting Apart*. That same week, Ansonia separated from Derby to form its own city. There were a number of issues between the communities, but one bone of contention was the Sterling Opera House, which also doubled as a city hall that some vainly hoped would serve a greater city composed of the boroughs of Birmingham, Ansonia, and Shelton, along with the town of Derby, on its lower floors. Sterling's days as an entertainment center and meeting place were long gone when city hall moved out in 1965. Vacant since then, Sterling's exterior has recently been renovated, and its long silent interior awaits restoration to reclaim its former importance to Derby.

CITY HALL & OPERA HOUSE, DERBY, CONN.

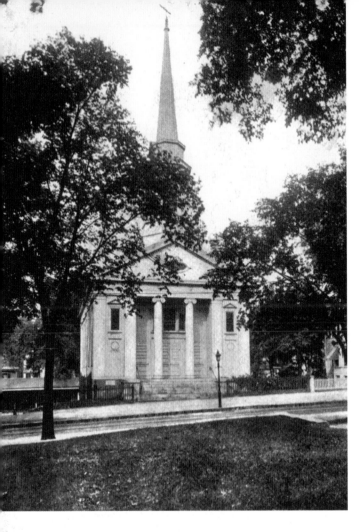

J ust above the Sterling is the Second Congregational Church, built on Elizabeth Street in 1846. The above photograph was taken from the green. Note the young trees and the gaslights. The basement of the church was used for a number of town gatherings in the 19th century. The anti-alcohol Derby Total Abstinence Society was organized here in 1847. The following year, Gen. Tom Thumb, P. T. Barnum's famous "man in miniature," performed here. The Second Congregational Church remains today, though the top of its steeple was toppled in Hurricane Gloria in 1985 and was not replaced.

The Irving School was built on the site of the former Birmingham Academy on the corner of Olivia and Fifth Streets in 1869. The top floor served as the high school for many years; its original class was five students. It was once said the building was solid enough to stand 1,000 years. It actually stood for 85 years and was razed not long after it closed for the last time in February 1954. The current buildings at the site, city hall (built in 1965) and a corner gas station, betray no hint of the generations of Derby schoolchildren who were educated here.

High School. Derby, Conn.

Elizabeth Street, Derby, Conn. 202,712. (J.V.)

Looking up Elizabeth Street at Fifth Street, the above photograph was taken after 1894 since the brick side of the new Methodist Episcopal (now Derby Methodist) church is present. The first Methodist Episcopal church was built on Fifth Street in 1837, and it was the first church on the green. Note the corner fire hydrant and storm drain has not moved in over 100 years. St. Mary's Roman Catholic Church, once completely obscured by the trees that lined Elizabeth Street (as seen in the *c.* 1900 postcard above), is now visible from the same vantage point in the lower photograph.

St. Mary's, the first Roman Catholic church in the valley, was erected on land donated by Anson Phelps in 1845. The present church, near the same spot, was dedicated in 1883. The convent to the right of the church in the photograph below was erected in 1904, and the school at the corner of Elizabeth and Cottage Streets was completed in 1898. The school served as an emergency hospital for Derby, Ansonia, and Shelton during the influenza epidemic of 1918. The convent and school were razed in 1969, and the space is now a parking lot. Not visible in either photograph is the rectory, out of view on the other side of the church. A fire severely damaged the rectory on November 10, 2003.

ST. MARY'S CHURCH, CONVENT AND SCHOOL, DERBY, CON

Elizabeth Street was tree-lined when this postcard of the "residential section" of Derby was made. The photograph to the left, taken at the same spot, reveals that the trees have long since given way to utility poles. This section of Elizabeth Street is just below and opposite the Derby Public Library. In 1958, the Beth Israel Synagogue Center was constructed beyond the Victorian home in the foreground. The congregation was formed in 1905, and the first synagogue was built in 1918 on Anson Street. The building is now the New Life Community Church.

Edward N. Shelton's mansion, built in 1845, was a landmark at the junction of Elizabeth and Caroline Streets and Seymour Avenue. As president of the Ousatonic Water Company, Shelton oversaw the construction of the Ousatonic Dam on the Housatonic River in 1870 and the canals that radiate from each side. The canal on the west bank of the Housatonic gave rise to a whole new industrial city, which was named Shelton in his honor. The mansion was razed in 1953 to make room for the New Irving School. It is now simply called the Irving School, but some Derby residents had proposed naming the new facility Greystone School while it was under construction.

Elizabeth Street ends at Seymour Avenue, though the latter street continues all the way to the Ansonia line. The Unitarian church was built at the corner of Seymour and Atwater Avenues. The church disbanded by 1922, and the John H. Collins American Legion Post No. 24 rented the building. A citizens committee purchased the building in 1927, and it was renamed the Veterans' Memorial Home for the use of all Derby veterans groups. This arrangement continues today. A cannon was later added, and the nation's first chapter of the Military Order of the Purple Heart dedicated a memorial here on August 7, 2002. The Military Order of the Purple Heart was organized in Ansonia in 1932, and this most exclusive of veterans groups held its first national convention at the Sterling Opera House in October 1933.

For centuries, what was once called Old Town Road was just a sleepy country lane. That did not change even when the industrial sections of Ansonia and Birmingham were formed above and below it. The road assumed critical importance in 1889, however, when it became the border between Derby and newly independent Ansonia, and it was aptly renamed Division Street. This c. 1925 view looks up the hill from what will later become the street's intersection with Pershing Drive.

Chapter 4

DIVISION
STREET

The east end of Division Street terminates just over the Naugatuck River, near the heart of Derby's pre-industrial settlement. On the Derby side of the corner of Division Street and Derby Avenue is Gen. William Hull's house. An uncle to Commo. Isaac Hull, General Hull served with distinction in the Revolutionary War. Charged with defending Detroit in the War of 1812, Hull surrendered the outpost rather than fight a costly battle he could not win. For this he was tried for treason and sentenced to death, but appeals from his Revolutionary War comrades and others forced a reexamination of Hull's actions, resulting in the exoneration of all charges. Now used by businesses, Hull's home remains, unlike Claude Bartelame's 1760 saltbox that was next door on Derby Avenue.

Opposite the General Hull house, Division Street turns into Elm Street, which lies completely in Ansonia. The trolley tracks in the foreground are part of the belt line between Derby and Ansonia. Ansonia's Main Street is to the left, while Derby Avenue lies in the other city to the right. Claude Bartelame (Bartholomew) built the house in the foreground for his son Jerrod in 1793. The fence across the street belonged to the Josiah Smith house, built in 1798. The traffic triangle still exists today, and the entire length of Elm Street, including the Bartelame and Smith houses, became the Ansonia Historic District in 1969.

Old Town Road, Derby, Conn.

There were actually two bridges to cross between General Hull's house and the steep hill on Division Street in the 1800s. The road crossed the Naugatuck River and then went through Derby Meadows. After the Meadows was the causeway over the old Birmingham Canal (above), built in the 1830s. The canal was filled in the 1920s, though the area remained underdeveloped until the new Mill Street Connector was built in the mid-1950s, linking with the Commodore Hull Bridge over the Housatonic and for a time extending Route 8 along this thoroughfare. The connector first appears as Pershing Drive in the local directories in 1962, and businesses now line it and Division Street around this busy intersection.

This view shows the quiet intersection of Division Street and Mill Street–Pershing Drive, looking toward the Naugatuck River. The fact the canal appears to have been recently filled in (note the earthmoving equipment on the horizon) indicates the photograph below was taken in the 1920s. The barely visible house in the right foreground was torn down in 1998 to make way for a major re-grading of the steep Division Street hill. The fields of Derby Meadows in the background were used for cattle pasture, a horse racing track, a drive-in movie theater, and other uses requiring a lot of land over the years.

The Halfway House was located in Ansonia, at the corner of Division Street and Clifton Avenue. This house was the famous, or infamous, home of Squire Booth, a land speculator who purchased this old home and attaching farm. As Anson Phelps tried to expand Birmingham north, Booth continued to raise his price. Unfortunately, he raised it too high for Phelps's taste, causing him to abandon the expansion project in favor of establishing a new factory village up the river bearing the name Ansonia, a Latinized version of his first name, changing the course of the region's history. The home was torn down years ago, and a new one was built in its place. Left of the Halfway House is the old Downing's Fish Market, which burned in 2003.

St. Mary's second Catholic cemetery was established on what is now the Ansonia side of Division Street in 1883. Off to the right, in front of the cemetery, is Grove Street, and Ansonia's Wakelee Avenue also branches to the right, behind the cemetery. On the left is the Baldwin-Sobin home. Built by Revolutionary War veteran Dr. Silas Baldwin *c.* 1758, the house was the residence of former Ansonia mayor Sturgis Sobin (1971–1973), who also ran an antique business here, in the 20th century. Now partly obscured by a pine tree, the Baldwin-Sobin home, built *c.* 1758, remains today on Seymour Avenue on the Derby side. St. Mary's first cemetery was founded in 1847 a bit farther up Wakelee Avenue at Burton Street. The area was called Baldwin's Corners in the 19th century.

Looking down Seymour Avenue at Division Street in front of the Baldwin-Sobin home, one is struck by how barren the landscape at the Derby and Ansonia border was, even in the early 1900s, when this photograph was taken. Appearances could be deceptive, however, since Griffin Hospital, formed in 1909 to serve the valley towns, was located just beyond the horizon, on the opposite side of the street from the Baldwin-Sobin home. Since then, a number of businesses and professional offices have been built along Seymour Avenue to support the valley's only general hospital.

Like Birmingham, Ansonia owed its existence to a canal that ran parallel to the Naugatuck River that powered its factories. Unlike Birmingham, Ansonia was not located on the edge of Derby or constrained by two rivers, so it had a much easier time expanding. Ansonia's Main Street was laid out in 1840s upon relatively flat terrain and was designed to support industrial, commercial, and residential buildings. In 1849, the *Derby Journal* was already lamenting the competition between Ansonia and Birmingham, which led to Ansonia's independence exactly 50 years later. This *c.* 1950 aerial view shows Ansonia's how Main Street (in the center, in front of Holy Rosary Church) was built between the river and the power canal. The canal is visible halfway up Main, one block to the right.

Chapter 5

MAIN STREET, ANSONIA

AERIAL VIEW, CITY of ANSONIA, CONN
Photo Fred Haverly

The photograph above shows the corner of Main and Platt Streets, looking south toward Columbia Street c. 1895. The area was once a thriving working-class neighborhood. Every structure in this photograph has been replaced by the wider Main Street and the businesses seen in the photograph to the left. The redevelopment in the 1960s leveled whatever buildings survived the 1955 flood, removing all residences from this area. Platt Street was discontinued at Vine Street at this time, no longer intersecting with Main Street.

The photograph below was taken at the same time as the one on the previous page, looking north toward what was then the Holy Rosary Church, originally the first edifice for the Church of the Assumption, Ansonia's first Roman Catholic church. Once teeming with small stores and apartment buildings, this section of Main Street was hit particularly hard by the flood of 1955. The surviving buildings, including the church, seen in to the right in a photograph taken a little farther up at Main and Front Streets *c.* 1960 by Vincent "Jim" Giammario of Ansonia, were torn down in the mid-1960s for redevelopment.

Vincent Giammario took the above photograph on the corner of Main and Platt Streets, looking toward Front Street. The contrast is startling. Even though the photographers are standing nearly on the same spot, only two generations apart, absolutely nothing from the earlier photograph exists in the newer. Even the intersections are gone; Platt Street no longer runs this far, and the east side of Front Street became part of Father Salemi Drive during the redevelopment in the 1960s. This section of Main Street is now wider, faster, and busier, with absolutely no trace of the structures, and the lives they sheltered, that were present for well over 120 years before the redevelopment.

This rather unique view of the rear of Holy Rosary Church was taken by Vincent Giammario near East Main Street, looking down Cheever Street toward Main Street. Finding the location where Giammario stood is difficult today, as both Holy Rosary and Cheever Street were eradicated by redevelopment c. 1965 for the new Ansonia Mall. The mall proved less than successful, and it was razed in 1997 to make way for a new supermarket. The upper view shows about where the church and Cheever Street were, part of the parking lot of what is now the Big Y supermarket.

Redevelopment along Main Street also eliminated the one-way Tremont Street between West Main and Main Streets. The west corner of Main and Tremont Streets and every building in this photograph taken in the 1960s by Vincent Giammario, like so many other old Main Street scenes south of here, is now completely gone. The building in the right foreground housed another branch of the A&P in 1963, while the large building across Tremont housed the Schoonmaker Drug Store, the Ansonia Watch Hospital, and the Thrifty Poultry Market.

This is how Tremont Street, looking east from Main Street, appeared in the 1920s. The block was primarily residential, but Fred Zander's automobile supply and battery store and J. J. Heffernan's plumbing and heating business appear on the right side. East Main Street did not exist yet, as the Ansonia Canal still ended behind the buildings on the left in the 1920s. The road, just behind and to the right of the truck was called Factory Street, though that was later incorporated into East Main Street after it was built over the canal. So treacherous was the Tremont Street hill in the background that it often was closed in the winter. Now a one-way lane, Tremont Street marks the boundary of the radical redevelopment that affected the southern section of Main Street.

The above view of Main Street, south of Bridge Street, from the 1950s offers one last glance at that southern Main Street before its redevelopment. In the lower photograph, some of the buildings on the left still exist today. Riordan's (a department store), Young Folks Clothing, the Endicott Johnson shoe store, and the Rose Flower Shops have long since departed Main Street, although Eddy's Bake Shop is still in business at a different location. The building in the right foreground was called the Kornblut Block, and it housed the Henry Kornblut store. The two-story brick building just beyond it was once called the Hotel Ansonia.

One of Ansonia's premier stores when this photograph was taken *c.* 1895, the Boston Store was located on the corner of Main and Bridge Streets. The three-story brick building in the background was a harbinger of things to come, as every wood structure seen in this photograph was gradually replaced by brick blocks. The Boston Store sold "dry and fancy goods" according to a 1904 advertisement. In 1907, it boasted itself as "the shopping mart of Ansonia and vicinity." Next door was the Ansonia Market. The view to the right shows that the corner, just below Bridge Street, bears absolutely no resemblance to its prior appearance.

This is a view of Bridge Street, looking west from Main Street, in the aftermath of the blizzard of 1888. The covered bridge that crossed the Naugatuck River at Bridge Street is visible in the background, just below the white house in the center of the photograph. The covered bridge was later replaced by a more contemporary span. After some wrangling, the state took over what was called the Bridge Street Bridge in July 1954; while it was kept open to traffic, it was legally closed so a survey could be done on the bridge's condition. Soon after, the Bridge Street Bridge and virtually every other span across the Naugatuck River was washed away in the flood of 1955. Note that the rebuilt bridge is raised high over the river to prevent its being damaged by a similar calamity.

The photographer who took the picture on the previous page also took the photograph below, a bit farther down Bridge Street, looking east. Bridge Street ended at Main Street in 1888 at the original copper mill built by Phelps and Dodge in 1844 in background. So confident was Anson Phelps's possibilities that he began building the mill before construction even began on the Ansonia Canal, the source of its power. After East Main Street was built over the canal, Bridge Street was extended directly over the site once occupied by the copper mill.

In 1905, the Murray Block, seen in the left foreground in the 1920s view above, was constructed on the spot that once housed the Boston Store. The Boston Store continued in its old location, operating out the Murray Block until it closed during the Great Depression. The Murray Block was destroyed by fire in 1987, and the site is now Haddad Park. The Capitol Building at 270-290 Main Street was built in 1920. It was home to a number of businesses over the years, but its best remembered tenant was the Capitol Theatre. The last year the Capitol appeared in local directories was 1968.

The building that housed a brewing company (seen in the left foreground of the 1903 view below), at the corner of Main and Water Streets, still exists more than 100 years later, though it has been altered somewhat. Just out of view on the right is Ansonia City Hall. The building with the rounded turret on the right was the Ansonia Clock Company, which replaced an earlier factory that burned down in 1854. Although the firm moved out of Ansonia in 1881, the Ansonia Clock Company building still exists today. Note the streetlight on the corner in the 1903 photograph and compare it to the modern ones. A carbon arc light, invented by Ansonia resident William Wallace in the 1870s, is above the intersection in the lower view. Carbon arc lights were harshly bright and painful to view directly.

MAIN STREET, ANSONIA, CONN.

Both the Ansonia City Hall, part of which is in the extreme right corner of the above photograph, and the Sentinel Building, to city hall's left, were constructed in 1905. Founded in 1871, the *Evening Sentinel* ceased publishing in 1992, leaving the valley without its own daily newspaper ever since. The post office, with its white columns, was constructed in 1914. The large building beyond in the above photograph was part of the American Brass Company. Built in 1962, the former Ansonia Savings Bank, at the corner of Main Street and Kingston Drive, was one of the first new buildings erected in downtown Ansonia after the 1955 flood. A relatively new street, Kingston Drive started appearing in local directories in 1964.

Trolley tracks for the electric Derby Street Railway Company and the Birmingham and Ansonia Horse Railroad Company were laid on the upper part of Main Street in 1887. The lines merged in 1890. The fact that a single track appears in the below photograph indicates the photograph was taken after the merger. The west side of Main Street, looking north before and after Maple Street, has changed little in the past century. The Farrel Foundry still occupies the land, where it has been producing metal goods and machinery since 1847.

The same photographer who took the photograph on the previous page took the photograph above, this time looking south down Main Street, just above Maple Street. The *Evening Sentinel* was still publishing out of the Gardella building in the corner building on the right, indicating the photograph was taken before 1905. The building below it was called Smith's H. J. Block, followed by the Hotchkiss Block, the Steele Block, Terry Block No. 2, Terry Block No. 1, and the Ansonia Opera House. All exist today. The opera house was built in 1870, and though its days of hosting touring companies lasted less than a generation, it continued to serve Ansonia's people as a venue for meetings, dances, movies, socials, and even basketball and roller-skating.

Republican James C. Blaine roars across the Maple Street Bridge onto Main Street while campaigning in Connecticut for the 1884 presidential election. While attracting a sizable crowd in Ansonia, Blaine eventually lost the close election to Democrat Grover Cleveland. A mere footbridge when it first started appearing on local maps by 1856, the bridge Blaine crossed was a covered bridge, though it was replaced by a more modern span by 1900. The bridge was destroyed during the flood of 1955, when the private Brass Company Bridge upstream was torn from its abutments and smashed into the Maple Street span, collapsing it. The new bridge, seen in the upper photograph, was completed in 1957 and renamed the Veteran's Memorial Bridge.

Dominated by Farrels, the very top of Main Street was called Foundry Hill. Still surrounded by the same wrought-iron fence, the building in the right foreground continues its original use today as the Farrel Corporation's main offices. Above that is the Eagle Hose Hook and Ladder Company No. 6 firehouse. Formed in 1887, the fire company has occupied this 1 Main Street firehouse since 1905. The Baptist church was built in 1881 but is no longer used. East Main Street does not exist between the church and firehouse in the top photograph. In the background, the Ansonia Armory, built in 1921 and sold to the city in 2004, appears on the same knoll the Slade estate once occupied at 5 State Street.

South Cliff Street was a rather unique suburb of downtown Ansonia. While it paralleled Main Street, a steep bluff allowed only road access from State and Tremont Streets in the 1800s, both of which were on steep hills and not centrally located. The grand Cliff Walk was constructed out of wooden stairs, platforms, and a footbridge over the Ansonia Canal that allowed access from the heart of South Cliff Street to the heart of Main Street. Thus, a busy pedestrian walk closely linked two vital and distinct parts of town. Lined with middle- and upper-class homes, South Cliff Street was a desirable neighborhood.

Chapter 6
SOUTH CLIFF STREET

South Cliff Street, Ansonia, Conn.

06335

Clara Barton Drew (1867–1946) moved to New Street, a short lane between South Cliff and Mott Streets, after she was married in 1888. Drew was a rare female professional photographer in the early 20th century, and she took the photograph above. The woman seated on the porch, second from left, is her namesake, Clara Barton, the founder of the American Red Cross. Barton visited Ansonia several times to call upon Drew. Nearly a century later, Drew's home and the rest of her New Street neighborhood are relatively unchanged.

Clara Barton Drew likely took the picture below. The view looks toward Drew's home, which is a block down New Street. The right fork is Mott Street, and the left fork is Cottage Street. Although some cosmetic differences exist between the two photographs (namely, the absence of pines in the older photograph and the absence of elms in the present-day picture), most of the actual structures have changed remarkably little in the past century.

A motorist and his passengers stop to pose for Clara Barton Drew's camera with their newfangled automobile on the corner of New and Mott Streets on their way to South Cliff Street in the early 20th century. A more modern car appears in the same spot about a century later. Note the two homes in the background in both pictures. They are joined by a post–World War II ranch-style home in the present-day photograph. The road to the left of the first house is Garden Street.

Waterbury native Frederick L. Gaylord built this house at 69 South Cliff Street, next door to the Ansonia Library, in the 1870s. He owned the F. L. Gaylord Company, founded in 1886, on 28 Pleasant Street. An 1890 account states the company manufactured "fine light and heavy castings in brass, bronze, composition and German silver." He was also a bookkeeper for Wallace and Sons and was once a postmaster. The library was built in 1881 and dedicated the following year. Note the four-horsepower carriage in the photograph below and the substantially more powerful horseless carriage in the present-day view.

Those who ascended the Cliff Walk from Main Street were greeted with this view at its South Cliff Street summit. The walk actually took one between the Christ Episcopal Church (not shown) and the Ansonia Congregational Church (on the left). The Congregational church was organized in 1850, and the present edifice dedicated in 1865. Across South Cliff, at its junction with Prospect Street, is the Ansonia High School, reconstructed in 1890 from a smaller school built in 1862 and destroyed by fire in 1932. The house on the right, at the corner of Cottage and Prospect Streets, is the Congregational parsonage, while the watering trough that remains today in front of Ansonia Library sits between the high school and parsonage on the fork at South Cliff and Cottage Streets.

At the corner of South Cliff and State Streets stood the Theodore P. Terry house, built in the 1860s. The house, which actually stood at 40 State Street, did not fare as well as the two Terry Blocks that remain a few blocks below on Main Street. Theodore P. Terry and Son sold hardware, stoves, "house furnishing goods," and steam and gas fittings and also engaged in plumbing. Like many of Ansonia's grand old homes, it has since been torn down, and the site is now a parking lot.

The grandest home in Ansonia of yesteryear was Tower Hall, the home of Franklin Farrel, son of Farrel Foundry owner Almon Farrel, diagonally across State and South Cliff Streets from the Terry House, on North Cliff and State Streets. The house was built before 1888 and underwent a number of renovations over the next few decades that altered its appearance considerably. Farrel died here in 1912. The home shared the fates of many other large Ansonia houses that were difficult to heat and maintain, and it was razed. Smaller houses occupy the site today, and North Cliff has changed much in the past century. A Masonic lodge lies just beyond the former Franklin estate in the lower photograph, and a parish school, built in 1910, now complements Assumption Church.

This was the view so familiar to generations of Ansonia residents, who used the Cliff Walk to go to work, school, and church, to shop, or to just get from Main Street to South Cliff Street. Lined with iron rails, the wood and cement stairs and platforms descend to the bridge over the Ansonia Canal to a covered alleyway between the Osborne and Cheeseman factories to Main Street in this *c.* 1926 photograph. East Main Street now covers the canal, and the stairs now end on its curb, but the alleyway remains. Formed in 1847, Osborne and Cheeseman moved to Ansonia from Birmingham in 1859. The Osborne and Cheeseman Company stopped appearing in the local directories in 1951. Part of the complex is now the Ansonia Senior Center.

Chapter 7

AROUND
ANSONIA

The above photograph shows the broken buildings, streets, cars, and lives in the immediate aftermath of the flood of August 19, 1955, called Black Friday by local residents. Vincent Giammario took this photograph on High Street, above Broad Street. High Street terminates in the distance where the front of what was the three-story Vartelas Building at 6 Maple Street, housing the Family Food Market and apartments, faces the intersection. In the rebuilding that followed, this section of High Street became part of the Olsen Drive Housing Complex. The sign just past the right corner, in front of the now unobstructed view of Farrel's below, is located exactly where the Vartelas Building once stood.

The collapsed Maple Street Bridge lies in the foreground, along with the shattered Vartelas Building across the river. The front of the white three-story building was at the corner of High and Maple Streets. Note the swath cut into the short dead-end lane called River Road by the floodwaters. None of the buildings along this section of the Naugatuck River's west bank in 1955 exist today. Vartelas Park was dedicated on the site of the Vartelas Building in 1987. A sign tells the story to later generations what those who lived through the flood of 1955 can never forget. John Vartelas's son, Jeremiah, is currently the president of the Derby Historical Society.

The above Vincent Giammario photograph of Farrel, the wrecked Maple Street Bridge, and the rear of Main Street illustrates why the 1955 flood was so devastating. The photograph to the left shows the pains Ansonia and the federal government took to prevent a similar calamity from happening again. There were virtually no effective flood-control measures along the Naugatuck River in 1955, and in fact smaller floods had occurred before that time. After the devastation of 1955, the Army Corps of Engineers built the high flood walls seen in the present-day view. Even the Veteran's Memorial Bridge over Maple Street, the Edward Clancy Bridge at Bridge Street, and the Peter Hart Bridge over Division Street, all dedicated in 1957 to replace destroyed spans, are positioned higher over the river than their predecessors.

The postcard below shows Franklin Street, which runs between the end of Maple Street and Wakelee Avenue. As Ansonia expanded, it spread across the Naugatuck River, steadily climbing up the bluff to Wakelee Avenue. The new section was known for decades as West Ansonia, and before Ansonia separated from Derby, it was considered a distinct community in its own right. Today the area is better known as the West Side. Franklin Street was part of this desirable neighborhood. Today it is one of main arteries between downtown and Route 8, and photographers trying to re-create this postcard scene in the middle of the street do so at their own peril.

Franklin Street, Ansonia, Conn.

406336

The postcard above shows Wakelee Avenue at the corner of Franklin Street. This branch trolley track connected with the Derby-Ansonia belt line at Bridge and Lester Streets to High, Franklin, and Jackson Streets before reaching Wakelee Avenue. The working watering trough in the foreground right indicates horses were still in wide use at this time. The photograph to the left shows most of the homes from the earlier photograph still exist, though many have been modernized. The preferred mode of transportation when each photograph was taken has also changed.

Col. William B. Wooster constructed the Victorian at 142 Clifton Avenue. A prominent local attorney, Wooster helped found the Derby Gas and Electric Company in 1859, serving as president from 1871 until his death in 1900. He was also a Civil War veteran, serving as colonel of the 20th Regiment, Connecticut Volunteers. He was captured at Chancellorsville but was later exchanged and went on to fight at Gettysburg. His home was donated by his descendant, Gen. Charles Pine, to build the Charles Pine Manual Trade School, pictured in the photograph to the right, in 1923. The stone retaining wall that once supported the Wooster home, as well as one of its staircases, still

exists today. The school was renamed Pine-Willis School in 1970 and has since been closed.

This view shows the corner of Central Avenue and Beaver Street. At the corner was Stordy Sales and Service, whose round sign advertises Flying A service. Down the hill were Levine's Liquor Store and the Ansonia Bottling Works. Beyond was a junkyard that was composed mostly of scrap metal. Other buildings housed crowded apartments. Today the corner of Central Avenue and Beaver Street contains the Ansonia Housing Authority's John Stevens Senior Housing complex.

The large Charles F. Brooker House was built in the 1890s at the corner of State and Johnson Streets. Charles F. Brooker was the first president and leading architect of the creation of the American Brass Company, which united a number of brass factories from Ansonia, Waterbury, and Torrington. His wife was instrumental in preserving and moving the Rev. Mansfield House on Jewett Street in 1926, now owned by the Derby Historical Society. Like Tower Hall, Franklin Farrel's mansion next door, it proved difficult and expensive to maintain after the Brookers passed on, and the smaller houses seen above were later built on it site. The Brookers' ornate wall remains to this day.

Robert and Elizabeth Wood built this grand brick house *c.* 1887 at 91 North Cliff Street. Unfortunately, Robert Wood did not have much time to enjoy his new home, as he died in August 1890. He was a factory superintendent at the Wallace and Sons brass mill complex. After Elizabeth Wood's death, the home passed into the Tuttle family, and *c.* 1960 it became the Bennett Funeral Parlor, pictured to the left. Note that the carriage house in the above photograph has since been removed.

At first glance, these two photographs taken 40 years apart may seem to depict a home built after World War II, located at North Main Street near Byron Avenue not far from the Seymour town line. In fact, Capt. Nathaniel Johnson constructed the house in 1773. Johnson was part of one of the first contingents of Derby soldiers organized after the Battle of Bunker Hill during the American Revolution. Marian O'Keefe took both of these pictures.

The David Humphreys house, at 37 Elm Street, was built in 1698 for Rev. John James, who was also Derby's town clerk and first schoolmaster. The house was enlarged and rebuilt in 1733. Rev. Daniel Humphreys purchased the house *c.* 1735, becoming the third Congregationalist minister to reside there. His son, David Humphreys, aide-de-camp to George Washington as well as the nation's first ambassador, pioneer industrialist, and poet, was born here. For many years, the house was in possession of the Humphreys House Association, organized by several civic-minded persons interested in preserving it. The house was turned over to the Derby Historical Society in 1961. Marian O'Keefe took the above photograph in 1964, before the house was restored in 1980 to its appearance in the photograph below. Now open to the public, it serves as the historical society's headquarters.